Shadows and Reflections

Tana Hoban

Greenwillow Books, New York

Library of Congress Cataloging-in-Publication Data

Hoban, Tana.
Shadows and reflections / Tana Hoban.
p.   cm.
Summary: Photographs without text feature shadows and
reflections of various objects, animals, and people.
ISBN 0-688-07089-2. ISBN 0-688-07090-6 (lib. bdg.)
1. Shadows—Pictorial works—Juvenile literature.
2. Reflections—Pictorial works—Juvenile literature.
[1. Shadows—Pictorial works. 2. Reflections—
Pictorial works.] I. Title. TR654.H59 1990
779'.092—dc20 89-30461   CIP   AC

For Susan